Fun to Play
RECORDER

MARSHALL CAVENDISH

This edition exclusive to Chapters in Canada
Produced by Marshall Cavendish Books
(a division of Marshall Cavendish Partworks Ltd)

Copyright © Marshall Cavendish 1996

ISBN 1-85435-884-7

Printed in France

Some of this material has previously appeared in
the Marshall Cavendish partwork *Music Box*

Contents

ABOUT YOUR RECORDER

There are four main sizes of recorder. They are the tenor recorder (the biggest), treble, descant and sopranino (the smallest). The first four pages of this book are about the descant recorder.

Your recorder may be made of wood or plastic.

Fingerholes

Window **Lip**

Double holes

Body

Head

Foot

Mouthpiece

The lip is the opening in the head which produces the sound. It is fragile, so try not to touch it.

Joints Most recorders have two or three joints, or sections. They are the head joint, with the lip and mouthpiece, the middle joint or barrel, and the foot.

Assembling your recorder When fitting your recorder together or taking it apart, gently twist the joints as well as pushing or pulling them, or they may crack.

Making a sound

First try blowing your recorder without covering any of the holes: hold the head joint between your left thumb and first finger, and support the recorder underneath with your right thumb. Take a deep breath and blow gently and steadily into the mouthpiece. If the recorder squeaks, you're blowing too hard! **Tonguing** is using your tongue to make a crisp beginning to the notes. Try saying "too" as you blow into the recorder.

Back view

Front view

First notes
Now you are ready to play proper notes.

The first is B. Use your left thumb to cover the hole under the recorder. Cover the first hole on top with your left-hand first finger, as shown below.

Your second note is A. The fingering is the same as for B, but with your left-hand middle finger covering the second hole.

Fingering. The pictures above show where to put your fingers on the recorder. Your left hand goes on top, with your left thumb over the hole underneath the recorder, and your first three left-hand fingers covering the top three holes. The left-hand little finger is not used. Now the right hand, with your thumb underneath, supporting the recorder, and your four fingers covering the last holes.

B

A

Covering the keys

To check if you are playing the recorder correctly, look at your hands when you have finished; there should be clear marks on the **centre** of each finger, with the left thumb mark on the side.

The next note is G. The fingering is the same as for A, but with the third finger of your left hand covering the next hole. Practise B, A and G.

Top D is a high note. Play it with all your fingers raised, except the second finger of your left hand. Your left thumb is raised too.

For top C, put your second left-hand finger down and cover the hole under the recorder with your left thumb. Practise all the notes you've learned.

G

top D

top C

E is a low note. Cover holes with your left fingers and thumb and the next two holes with the first two fingers of your right hand. Blow very gently.

To play D, cover all the holes you did to play E. Now lower the third finger of your right hand to cover all of the first double hole.

Top E is played using the same fingers as for E, but with your left thumb bent so that it covers only part of the hole. This is called pinching.

E

D

top E

How a recorder works

When you blow into the mouthpiece of your recorder, you direct a stream of air against the sharp edge of the lip. Air flows alternately over the lip and inside the recorder. This causes air to vibrate inside the instrument, producing sound.

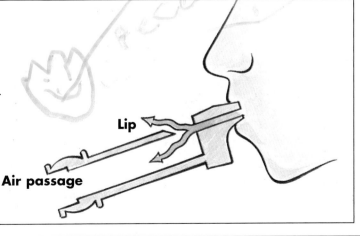

Lip

Air passage

Posture

Keep your back straight. Leave a small gap between your elbows and your body.

Whether you are sitting down or standing up, you need to feel comfortable when playing the recorder. Hold your head up straight and keep your shoulders down. Keep your body relaxed, including your shoulders, lips and mouth. Breathe deeply and steadily as you play. The girl would be more comfortable if her feet were flat on the floor!

Hold your recorder at roughly the angle shown here. If you don't have a music stand, prop your music up on a table with some books. Put the music at an angle so that you can read it comfortably.

F♯

top C♯

F

C

B♭

C♯

Low C is the recorder's lowest note. The fingering is the same as for D, but with your right-hand little finger covering the last double hole.

To play B flat, cover holes with your left thumb, first and third fingers, and with the first finger of your right hand. Keep practising until you get a clear note.

To play C sharp, use the same fingering as for C, but cover only one of the small holes with your right-hand little finger.

top
F

G#

top
F#

top
G

top
E♭

E♭

Looking after your recorder

Your recorder will last a long time if you take good care of it. Don't leave it in the sun or on a radiator where it could warp or crack. Store it in a bag to prevent it from getting clogged with dust.

Moisture builds up inside your recorder as you play. To dry it, first remove the head. Gently push your mop or cleaning rod and cloth into the tube and pull it through. To clear moisture from the head, blow into the mouthpiece while covering the window. Don't touch the lip.

Always clean your recorder after use. Use either a mop (shown left) or a cleaning rod with a soft, dry cloth threaded through (shown above).

Handy Hints

• Rest the mouthpiece of your recorder on your chin while practising the fingering of each note.

• Practise the notes in the groups shown on these pages, until you can change smoothly between notes.

• Fingers that are not covering the holes should only be raised slightly, so that they are ready to play.

Sergei Prokofiev

A fiery and eccentric composer, Prokofiev's "wrong-note" style and explosive rhythms established him as a bold new musical force.

Sergei Prokofiev (Prock-off-ee-eff) was born in the Ukraine in 1891 to comfortably-off parents. His mother played the piano and encouraged him to play from an early age. When he was five he picked out a tune on the keyboard which his mother wrote down – four years later he wrote both the music and libretto for a three-act opera called *The Giant*.

When he was 13, Sergei went to live in St Petersburg with his mother so that he could become a student at the music conservatory, under Rimsky-Korsakov. Here he started making his strange experiments with harmony.

In 1918 Prokofiev went to America, where he met his first wife, a young soprano called Lina Llubera. He spent the next 18 years as an exile – mostly in Paris – earning his living as a composer and concert pianist. He returned to Russia in 1936, and remained there for the rest of his life.

Key Facts

Sergei Prokofiev
1891-1953

NATIONALITY
Russian

APPEARANCE
Long oval face, thick lips and a "naughty boy" expression

CHARACTER
Self-confident, optimistic and a hard worker

St Petersburg Conservatory of Music, where Prokofiev was a music student.

SNAPSHOTS

Sergei was very fond of chess, which he learned to play when he was seven. Feeling bored one day, he insisted that the maid was let off work so that he could teach her to play!

A music tutor engaged to teach the 11-year-old Sergei won him over by accepting a challenge to fight a duel with toy pistols.

As a young man Prokofiev was nicknamed "The Martian" by his friends because of his eccentric behaviour and outlandish, foppish clothes.

Prokofiev was obsessed with making lists. When he was a student he started making lists of all the mistakes made by his fellow students in the harmony class – which did not make him at all popular!

LES RIDICULES

KEY: C

A lighter note

Prokofiev's Second Piano Concerto caused chaos at its première – a critic said it sounded like "dusting the keys". Some people left the hall, others hissed, and some cried "the cats at home can make music like this!"

Bedřich Smetana

Smetana's life was full of struggle, but he never abandoned his goal of writing music that would put his homeland on the map.

Bedřich Smetana (Smet-anna) was born in Bohemia in 1824. His father started to teach him the violin when he was four, and he made such good progress that he soon began piano lessons too. But despite youthful successes in composition and performance, Bedřich had no music lessons from age 12 to 19.

As soon as he left school, he took odd jobs so that he could devote himself to playing, composing and learning theory from books. Later he got a job as resident piano teacher to a count in Prague, which meant he could pay for music lessons for himself.

In 1848 Smetana set up a music school and the following year married Kateřina, his childhood sweetheart.

His "dangerous" modern music continued to arouse much hostility, but Smetana never gave up his struggle to compose truly nationalistic Czech music.

Carol singers round the St Wenceslas statue in Prague, where Smetana lived.

Key Facts

Bedřich Smetana
1824-1884

NATIONALITY
Czech

APPEARANCE
Short, with thick, dark hair and a kindly expression

CHARACTER
Sensitive, emotional and determined

THE MOLDAU

KEY: A MINOR

E   A   B   C   D   E   E   E

F   F   E   E   D   D   D

C   D   C   C   B   B   A   E

A   B   C   D   E   E   E   F   F   E   E

D   D   D   C   D   C   C   B   B   A

A lighter note

The young Smetana loved dancing, particularly the energetic polka. He was in great demand as a partner at local dances held on the village green as he could out-dance everyone else!

Alexander Borodin

Borodin was one of the "Mighty Handful" of 19th-century Russian composers who wrote colourful music spiced with folk tunes.

Alexander Borodin was the illegitimate son of a Russian prince, who had the infant registered in the name of one of his serfs. Alexander was brought up by his mother (whom he always called "Auntie") in St Petersburg. He learned to play the piano, flute and cello, and started to compose at an early age. He also developed a passion for chemistry, and from the age of 14 conducted experiments in a laboratory he made in his home.

Sasha (as he was called by his family and friends) studied and qualified as a doctor, but was never really suited to the medical profession. He eventually became a professor of chemistry but music remained a vital part of his life. He and his friends Mussorgsky, Balakirev, Cui

and Rimsky-Korsakov were known as the "Five" or "Mighty Handful" of nationalist composers. He married a concert pianist, Catherine Protopopova, in 1863.

Key Facts

Alexander Borodin
1833-1887

NATIONALITY
Russian

APPEARANCE
Dark hair, noble brow and intelligent, piercing eyes

CHARACTER
Friendly, open-hearted and a witty conversationalist

St Petersburg, where Borodin lived.

As a small boy Borodin enjoyed visiting the local parade ground with his nurse to hear the military band play. He would talk to the bandsmen, study their instruments, and pick out on the piano at home the tunes they had played.

Borodin had a laboratory next to his apartment where he carried out chemical experiments. When he was playing music with friends he would often jump up and run into the laboratory to see whether something had burned out or boiled over.

Borodin kept open house and his four-room apartment was always overflowing with waifs and strays he had befriended, including four cats that would jump up on the table when people were eating, and leap on to the diners' backs.

DANCE OF THE YOUNG GIRLS

KEY: F

A lighter note

Borodin's laid-back attitude was the despair of his musical friends. When asked once if he had at last transposed a certain piece of music he replied, "Yes, I have. I transposed it from the piano to the table!"

Claude Debussy

Debussy created a new musical landscape – nicknamed "Debussyism" – that had a profound influence on 20th-century music.

After marrying Rosalie (Lily) Texier in 1899, Debussy's life seemed to settle down. He was just beginning to make his name as a composer – *Nocturnes* were first performed in 1901, followed in 1902 by his opera *Pelléas et Mélisande*.

Key Facts

Claude Debussy

1862-1918

NATIONALITY
French

APPEARANCE
Short, solidly built, with thick wavy black hair

CHARACTER
Shy and sensitive, with a mischievous sense of fun

But his life was thrown into confusion in 1903 when he met Emma Bardac, the mother of one of his pupils. Within a year they had eloped, and a year later their daughter, Chou-chou, was born. To support his new family Debussy undertook exhausting conducting tours, while still continuing to compose. His health began to give way, and in 1909 he learned that he had a life-threatening illness.

Nevertheless he went on working for the next nine years. He died in Paris in March 1918, towards the end of World War One, while the Germans were bombarding the city.

Paris as it looked to Debussy in the early years of the 20th century.

THE WIND AND THE SEA

KEY: C

F E F E F# E

F# E G G♭ F E E♭ D D♭ C

B B♭ A B♭ B B♭ A A♭ G G♭

F E D# E F E D# E

D♭ C B C D♭ F D♭ F

A lighter note

Trying to decide whether to accept the invitation of a hostess who wanted him to play for her as she sang, Debussy said, "She sings like a locomotive, but her buttered scones are marvellous!"

George Frideric Handel

A prolific composer of operas, oratorios and other music, Handel dominated the musical scene in the first half of the 18th century.

George Frideric Handel was born in Halle, Germany, in February 1685. Although the child showed a keen interest in music, his elderly father, a surgeon-barber, refused at first to allow him to play any

instrument. The story goes that the young Handel managed to smuggle a clavichord into the attic, and practised on it while the family was asleep! Persuaded eventually to allow the child to follow his talent, Handel's father paid for him to have lessons on the organ and harpsichord from a local organist, who also taught him harmony and gave him exercises to do in composition.

At 18, Handel joined the opera orchestra in Hamburg, playing violin and harpsichord, and the following year his first opera, *Almira*, was staged at the theatre, followed swiftly by his second, *Nero*. After several years in Italy, Handel visited London in 1712, and eventually settled there. He died in 1759.

Handel playing for the singer Mrs Cibber, from the film The Great Mr Handel.

Key Facts

George Frideric Handel

1685-1759

NATIONALITY
German first, then English

APPEARANCE
Heavily built, with a sombre, dignified expression

CHARACTER
Intelligent, witty and good-humoured

SNAPSHOTS

When the 19-year-old Handel and a friend started to fight a duel, a large metal coat button on Handel's coat deflected his friend's sword, and the composer's life was saved!

While walking in Marylebone Pleasure Gardens with a friend one day, Handel suggested they should sit down and listen to some music the band was playing. After a while his friend said, "It is not worth listening to – it is very poor stuff." "Yes, indeed," replied Handel, " I thought so myself when I had finished writing it!"

Although Handel lived in England for almost 40 years, and became a naturalized Englishman in 1726, he never lost his heavy German accent.

LA RÉJOUISSANCE

KEY: G

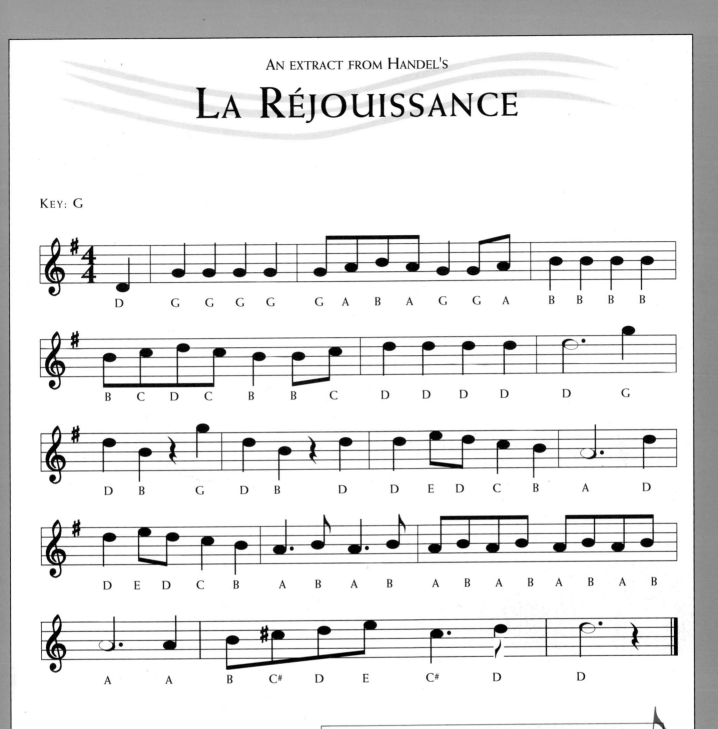

A lighter note

During an earthquake scare in London in 1749, many performances of Handel's new oratorio *Theodora* were almost empty. On these occasions he would console his friends by saying, "Never mind, the music will sound better!"

Igor Stravinsky

Stravinsky's music was new, dynamic and exciting – making a complete breakaway from 19th-century Romanticism.

Stravinsky was born in north-east Russia in 1882. He grew up in St Petersburg, where his father was leading bass singer at the opera house. The summers were spent visiting aunts and uncles in the country, and Igor's uncle Alexander, an amateur musician, encouraged the boy's love of music.

Igor started piano lessons at the age of nine, and later learned harmony and counterpoint. But his parents insisted that he study law at University. He started writing short piano pieces, and met Rimsky-Korsakov, who agreed to give him lessons.

In 1906 Stravinsky married his cousin, Catherine, and be-

gan making his mark as a composer. After the Russian Revolution in 1917, he and his family lived first in Switzerland, then France. Later he made his home in Hollywood, USA.

Key Facts

Igor Stravinsky
1882-1971

NATIONALITY
Russian, then French, then American

APPEARANCE
Short, with prominent features and a serious expression

CHARACTER
Enthusiastic, full of life, a hard worker

One of the main streets of 19th-century St Petersburg, where Stravinsky grew up.

AN EXTRACT FROM STRAVINSKY'S

DANCE OF THE PRINCESSES

KEY: F

A lighter note

Stravinsky's *Circus Polka* was a ballet for elephants! It was premièred in 1942 by the elephant troupe of the Barnum and Bailey Circus New York, who then proceeded to give more than 400 performances in all.

21

Wolfgang Amadeus Mozart

Insignificant to look at, Mozart was the supreme musical genius – immortal music poured out of him seemingly effortlessly.

Mozart (Mote-zart) was born in Salzburg into a musical family. His father Leopold was a court musician, and he taught young Wolfgang to play both violin and keyboard, as he had also taught his elder child, Nannerl. From a very early age the Mozart children were professional musicians. They toured the courts of Europe with their father,

playing concerts and earning their keep.

After making his name as a child prodigy, the adult Mozart continued composing and performing. In 1781 he moved from Salzburg to Vienna, and the following year married Constanze Weber, his landlady's daughter. The couple set up house in Vienna, where Mozart eventually gained an appointment as court composer to Emperor Joseph II in 1788.

Key Facts

Wolfgang Amadeus Mozart

1756-1791

NATIONALITY
Austrian

APPEARANCE
Short, pale, light-coloured hair, undistinguished

CHARACTER
Lively, witty, boisterous and full of energy

Salzburg in Austria, where Mozart was born in 1756.

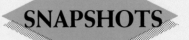

SYMPHONY NO.40

KEY: D MINOR

A lighter note

Visiting Mannheim, Mozart attempted to get in to a rehearsal of *The Marriage of Figaro*. The actor he asked thought he was a tailor's apprentice, and tried to have him thrown out of the theatre!

Sergei Rachmaninov

Rachmaninov was the last great Romantic composer of the 19th century – and also a famous concert pianist of the 20th century.

Sergei Rachmaninov (Rack-man-in-off) was born at Oneg in north-west Russia. Sergei showed early musical promise, and a teacher was engaged when he was six to give him piano lessons. When he was eight, his father lost all their money – they moved into a flat in St Petersburg, and his father left home and disappeared.

Sergei studied first at the St Petersburg Conservatory of Music and then the Moscow Conservatory. He started composing at 14, and wrote his opera *Aleko* in 15 days for

Rachmaninov (seated right) at 19 with his composition teacher Arensky (centre) and two other music graduates.

his final exam. After graduating he settled in Moscow, making a living by composing short piano pieces and teaching at a ladies' academy. In 1902 he married his cousin, Natalia Satin. Following the Russian Revolution in 1917 Rachmaninov left his beloved country, never to return.

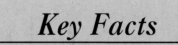

Key Facts

Sergei Rachmaninov

1873-1943

NATIONALITY
Russian

APPEARANCE
Dark hair, long face, quietly dressed

CHARACTER
Serious and reserved, but with a sense of humour

SNAPSHOTS

When Rachmaninov was a little boy, his mother's way of punishing him for being naughty was to make him sit under the piano.

As a schoolboy in St Petersburg Rachmaninov often played truant, and went to the ice skating rink instead.

Rachmaninov was the proud possessor of one of the first motor cars in Russia, and could often be seen driving it around the countryside with his uniformed chauffeur sitting beside him in the passenger seat.

At his family's country estate, everyone knew that if Rachmaninov was pacing the long avenue of trees known as the "red avenue" it meant he was composing, and no one must speak to him.

PIANO CONCERTO NO.2

KEY: D

A lighter note

After the première of the demanding Third Piano Concerto in New York in 1909, the enthusiastic audience wanted an encore. Rachmaninov held up his hands to show that while he was willing his hands were not!

Felix Mendelssohn

Mendelssohn was a child prodigy and in an eventful life he composed a wealth of sparkling, memorable music.

Felix Mendelssohn (Mendel-son) was born in Hamburg but his family moved to Berlin when he was two. His father was a banker and the family was wealthy. Felix was musically gifted, and he and his sister Fanny played the piano from an early age. He was educated at home, and started lessons in harmony at the age of eight. His early compositions were played at the Sunday morning musical parties his parents gave.

When he was 19 he embarked on a three-year tour of Europe, playing and composing along the way. He

Mendelssohn playing for the young Queen Victoria and Prince Albert.

returned to Germany and got work as musical director to various orchestras. He married Cecile Jeanrenaud, a beautiful French girl, when he was 28 and they had five children. Mendelssohn died at 38, only a few months after his beloved sister Fanny.

Key Facts

Felix Mendelssohn

1809-1847

NATIONALITY
German

APPEARANCE
Medium height, slim build and expressive features

CHARACTER
Full of vitality, outgoing and friendly

AN EXTRACT FROM MENDELSSOHN'S

HEBRIDES OVERTURE

KEY: B♭

Allegro

A lighter note

Conducting a rehearsal of Beethoven's *Egmont*, Mendelssohn was so enraged by the slovenly performance of the orchestra that he ripped the score in two and threw the pieces at the musicians!

Gustav Mahler

Mahler's music was never properly understood in his lifetime – but he is now recognised as an extraordinary musical genius.

Gustav Mahler (Mar-ler) was born in Bohemia on 7 July 1860, the second of 14 children. His childhood was not happy – the family was short of money, and his father, Bernhard, was a bully who beat his wife and children. However, Bernhard did pay for Gustav to have piano lessons, and later sent him to Prague and Vienna to study piano and composition.

After completing his studies, Mahler took a job as a conductor in a small opera house. His conducting career flourished, and he moved from one European city to another, earning a reputation for strictness and high standards of performance.

In 1901 he met Alma Schindler and within five months they were married. Mahler spent the last four years of his life in New York, but returned to Vienna in 1911 where he died.

Key Facts

Gustav Mahler
1860-1911

NATIONALITY
Austrian

APPEARANCE
Short, dark, with intense eyes behind wire-framed spectacles

CHARACTER
Insecure, dictatorial, but with a sense of humour

The Vienna Opera House, where Mahler was director of music for 10 years.

Mahler was not very practical. While he was out for a walk with his fiancée, his shoelaces kept coming undone and he had to stop every few minutes to retie them.

It was raining heavily on his wedding day, so Mahler walked to the church wearing galoshes.

When Mahler tried to ring home one day to say he would be late, he couldn't remember the number. He had to ring the Opera House where he worked and ask them what his home telephone number was.

Mahler loved the subway in New York, and while he was living there he would often refuse the offer from friends of a ride in a carriage or taxi in order to be able to travel on an underground train.

SYMPHONY NO.5

A lighter note

Staying as a guest in a private house, Mahler rushed out of his room one morning, kicking over a bucket of water at the top of the stairs – the water cascaded down, drenching his hostess who was standing below.

Johann Sebastian Bach

Bach's amazingly prolific output of inspired organ music has never been equalled and forms the basis of the organ repertoire to this day.

Bach (Bark) was born in Eisenbach, Germany, on 21 March 1685 into a musical family. Both his parents died while he was a child, and the 10-year-old Sebastian was brought up by his elder brother, Christoph. Christoph was organist at Ohrdruf, and he taught Sebastian to play and also perhaps showed him how to repair an organ.

At 15, Sebastian was sent 200 miles away to choir school at Lüneburg, where his board and tuition were free. His voice broke soon after his arrival, but he was kept on, possibly as an instrumentalist. At 18, after a brief spell as a court musician, he was given the post of organist

at a fine new church in Arnstadt. From then on, Bach spent his working life as a church organist or court composer. He married twice and had 20 children.

Key Facts

Johann Sebastian Bach

1685-1750

NATIONALITY
German

APPEARANCE
Medium height, square face, friendly expression

CHARACTER
Modest, hard-working, dedicated to music

Inside the house in Eisenbach where Bach was born over 300 years ago.

SNAPSHOTS

While he was a choirboy at Lüneburg, Bach made several trips (on foot) to Hamburg, 30 miles distant. On one trip he was resting outside an inn, tired and hungry, when someone threw out two herring heads. Bach picked them up and found that each head contained a gold piece – which enabled him to buy a good supper!

Bach was often asked to travel many miles to test and report on a new organ – to the alarm of the organ builder. Bach's way of testing an organ was to pull out all the stops and play it at maximum volume!

When he was director of music in Leipzig, Bach had to supervise the daily trips of eight choirboys to sing in neighbouring churches.

AN EXTRACT FROM J.S. BACH'S

TOCCATA AND FUGUE

KEY: E MINOR

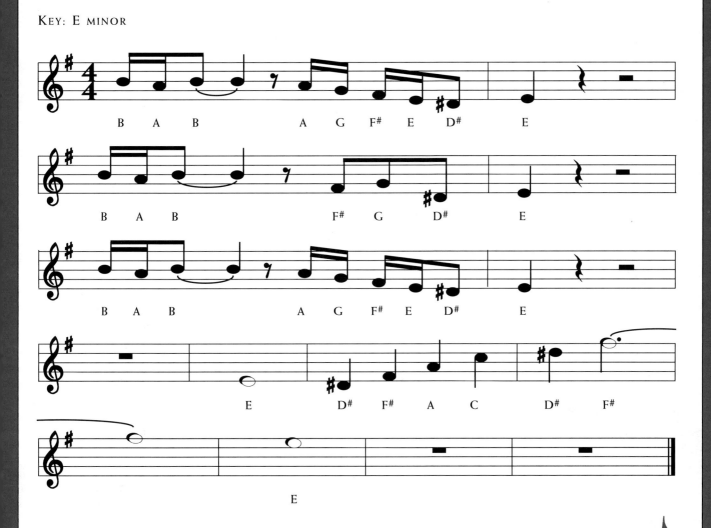

A lighter note

When Bach asked permission to leave his job with the Duke of Saxe-Weimar, his employer was so angry that he had Bach thrown into prison – where he languished a month before being released!

Ludwig van Beethoven

Beethoven was a truly titanic composer, and his prodigious works have influenced every composer since.

Beethoven (Bayt-hoven) was born in the small German town of Bonn, where his father and grandfather were court musicians. Life in the Beethoven household was not easy – money was short, and frequent visits were made to the pawn shop. But when his father started teaching little Ludwig to play the keyboard, the child made astounding progress. When he was seven his father took him to play at the court in Bonn – but in order to make the child's playing seem more impressive, his father gave his age as only five!

Ludwig left school at the age of 10, and from this time on he was a professional musician. At 21, he moved to

Vienna – where he remained for the rest of his life – and established himself as a teacher and composer. Within a few years he was the city's most respected musician.

Key Facts

Ludwig van Beethoven

1770-1827

NATIONALITY
German

APPEARANCE
Short, stocky, square-faced; often sloppily dressed

CHARACTER
Hardworking, determined, but given to bouts of depression

A view of Vienna, where Beethoven lived for most of his adult life.

RONDO

Key: G Minor

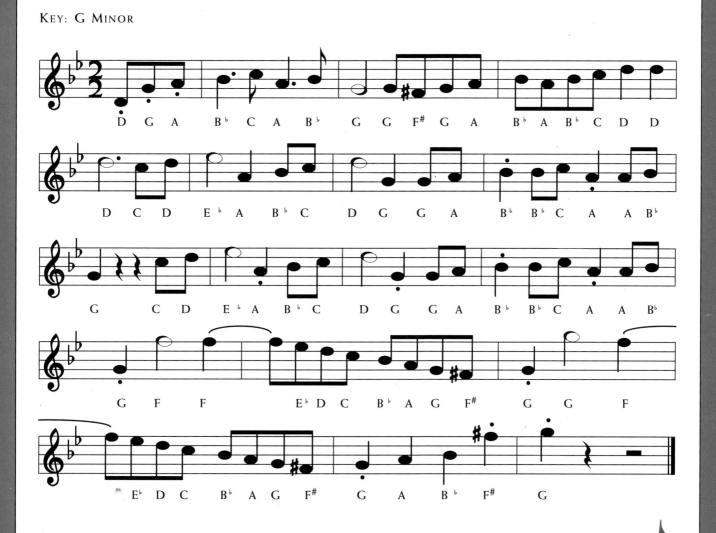

A lighter note

As a young man in Vienna, Beethoven went to many parties – but he never learned to dance properly. When he did dance, he constantly trod on his partner's feet – so the couple often tripped and fell over!

Franz Joseph Haydn

Haydn's witty, sparkling symphonies established the symphonic form and earned him the title of "Father of the Symphony".

SNAPSHOTS

Franz Joseph Haydn (High-dun) was born in Rohrau in Austria in 1732. His father was a wheel-wright, and the family was quite poor. When Joseph was six, his choir-master uncle noticed his remarkable musical talent, and took him away to sing in his choir. Two years later he won a place in the cathedral choir in Vienna.

When his voice broke, at 17, he was turned out of the choir school – destitute, with nowhere to go. He spent the first night on the streets. Happily an adult chorister found him next morning and took him home with him. For the next eight years Haydn scraped a living giving music lessons by day and teaching himself composition at night.

Eventually he was made assistant conductor (and later musical director) at the court of the Hungarian Prince Paul Esterházy, where he remained for the next 30 years.

The five-year-old Joseph improvised a toy violin to accompany family sing-songs by tucking a piece of wood under his chin and sawing away with a stick for a bow, keeping time with the music.

At the Esterházy court, Haydn had to present himself to the Prince every day at noon, dressed in court livery – white coat and knee breeches, white stockings and wig – to take his orders for the day.

When Haydn was in England Oxford made him an honorary doctor of music. At a concert the same evening, he wore his scarlet and cream doctor's gown, and was greeted with tumultuous applause. He bowed and said (in English) "I thank you." The audience shouted back, "You speak very good English!"

Key Facts

Franz Joseph Haydn

1732-1809

NATIONALITY

Austrian

APPEARANCE

Medium height, pock-marked skin, dark grey eyes

CHARACTER

Industrious and kind, with an infectious sense of fun

Haydn in Vienna in later life, when he had become a successful composer.

"SURPRISE" SYMPHONY

KEY: G

A lighter note

After one of Haydn's concerts in London the audience rushed forward in excitement. A glass chandelier fell and crashed where people had been sitting only moments before. Amazingly no one was hurt!

Wolfgang Amadeus Mozart

During his short life, Mozart wrote an enormous amount of music, some of it among the most beautiful ever written.

Mozart was a musical prodigy. From the age of six, he toured all the great cities of Europe with his sister Nannerl, playing before kings and princes in the all the grandest houses. He was also composing music during this time and by the age of 16 he had written well over 100 works.

For a while he worked alongside his father Leopold in Salzburg but soon he yearned for more freedom. He set off to look for work in Paris and then in Vienna. For a time he was paid very well for his compositions, performances and teaching. He married and he and his wife Constanze had six children. But they managed their money so badly that they

were always in debt. When Mozart died, aged just 35, there was not enough money for a decent funeral and he was buried in an unmarked, pauper's grave.

Key Facts

Wolfgang Amadeus Mozart

1756-1791

NATIONALITY
Austrian

APPEARANCE
Small, slight build, always fashionably dressed

CHARACTER
Full of wit and fun, fond of parties and high living

Mozart with his wife, Constanze, from the film Amadeus.

The six-year-old Mozart charmed his way through customs once by showing the customs officer his clavier, inviting him to visit, and playing him a minuet on his little fiddle. The customs officer waved the Mozart party through without inspecting their baggage!

When the 25-year-old Mozart was employed by the archbishop Colloredo, he had to eat at a table with the archbishop's servants, including two valets, a confectioner and two cooks.

Mozart was very fond of a game of billiards, and in two of his apartments he had a special billiards room in which he could play with his friends.

A LITTLE NIGHT MUSIC

AN EXTRACT FROM MOZART'S

KEY: C

Allegro

f   C   G   C   G   C   G   C E G   F   D   F   D

F D B D G   C   C   E D C   C B   B   D F B

D C C   E D C   C B   B   D F B C C   C B A B C C E D C D

E E G F E F G   *p*   G   A G F   F   F E E   E D D   C B A B

C   D   E   G   A   G F F F   F E E   E D D D C B A B C

A lighter note

Summoned to play at court, the six-year-old Mozart slipped on a polished floor and fell down. When a little girl helped him up, he said, "When I grow up I will marry you." She was Marie Antoinette, later Queen of France.

37

Glossary

clavichord A keyboard instrument which was very popular as a solo household instrument from the 16th to 18th century.

composition The creation of an original piece of music.

conductor The individual responsible for directing a musical performance using a baton or his or her hands.

counterpoint The combination of two or more independent lines of melody (a series of arranged notes varying in pitch), each of which is then said to be in *counterpoint* with the others.

Debussyism The nickname given to Debussy's musical style with its new forms of harmony and musical structure, which had a great influence on 20th-century music.

harmony A term used to describe the composition of chords in a piece of music: it refers to their structure, the way they balance each other, and how they develop in a musical work. A chord consists of three or more notes played together.

harpsichord A keyboard instrument similar to the piano, but with the strings made to sound by a plucking mechanism rather than by hammers as in a piano.

libretto In music libretto refers either to the text of a dramatic work, such as an opera or oratorio, or to the printed copy of such a text. Some composers write their own librettos; others employ writers to do it for them.

Mighty Handful Five Russian composers, including Borodin, who wrote nationalistic music.

nationalistic music A trend in musical composition which started at the end of the 19th century in which composers used the folk music and folk lore of their countries to influence their work, through which they could then express the spirit of their homeland.

opera A dramatic composition in which the characters sing rather than speak the text, accompanied by an orchestra. The music binds together the story, the themes, and the characterizations.

oratorio Today an oratorio is a large-scale concert work for solo singers, chorus and orchestra, usually on a serious subject.

organ A keyboard instrument using bellows to blow air through pipes which then make the sound of the notes being played on the keyboard.

patron The person, persons, or organization that asks a composer or artist to create a musical work or work of art. Usually the patron pays for the work.

prodigy A child of outstanding skill and accomplishment.

recorder The recorder is a member of the flute family. It has been played since medieval times.

repertoire The collection of pieces an individual or group is able to perform.

Romanticism The belief in the freedom of thought, the power of the imagination, and the importance of personal experience. Also the literary, artistic, and musical works that developed in response to this belief during the early 19th century.

score The written or printed copy of a musical work in which all the different parts belonging to the performers are combined in order.

symphony Since the time of Haydn, the term has come to mean a serious and large-scale orchestral work. Symphonies are usually divided into four sections called movements, which have different tempos (speeds) and create different moods and feelings for the audience.

We would like to thank Bill Lewington, London, for the kind use of

their musical equipment.